Maine

Facts and Symbols

by Emily McAuliffe

Consultant:
Connie Manter
Maine Department of Education
Augusta, Maine

Hilltop Books

an imprint of Capstone Press
Mankato, Minnesota

Hilltop Books are published by Capstone Press
818 North Willow Street, Mankato, Minnesota 56001
http://www.capstone-press.com

Library of Congress Cataloging-in-Publication Data
McAuliffe, Emily.
   Maine facts and symbols/by Emily McAuliffe.
   p. cm.—(The states and their symbols)
   Includes bibliographical references and index.
   Summary: Presents information about the state of Maine, its nickname, flag, motto,
and emblems.
   ISBN 0–7368–0376–9
   1. Emblems, State-Maine-Juvenile literature. [1. Emblems, State—Maine. 2. Maine.]
I. Title. II. Title: Maine. III. Series: McAuliffe, Emily. States and their symbols.
CR203.M35M38 2000
974.1—dc21   99-25111
                                                                               CIP

Editorial Credits

Damian Koshnick, editor; Heather Kindseth, cover designer; Linda Clavel, illustrator;
   Kimberly Danger, photo researcher

Photo Credits

Kevin Shields, 22 (middle)
Norlands Living History Center/Tony Castro, 22 (bottom)
One Mile Up Inc., 8, 10 (inset)
Robert McCaw, cover, 12, 14
Ron Thomas/FPG International LLC, 6
Root Resources/Kitty Kohout, 16; Pat Wadecri, 20
Unicorn Stock Photos/Andre Jenny, 22 (top)
Visuals Unlimited/Jeff Greenberg, 10; Hugh Rose, 18

Table of Contents

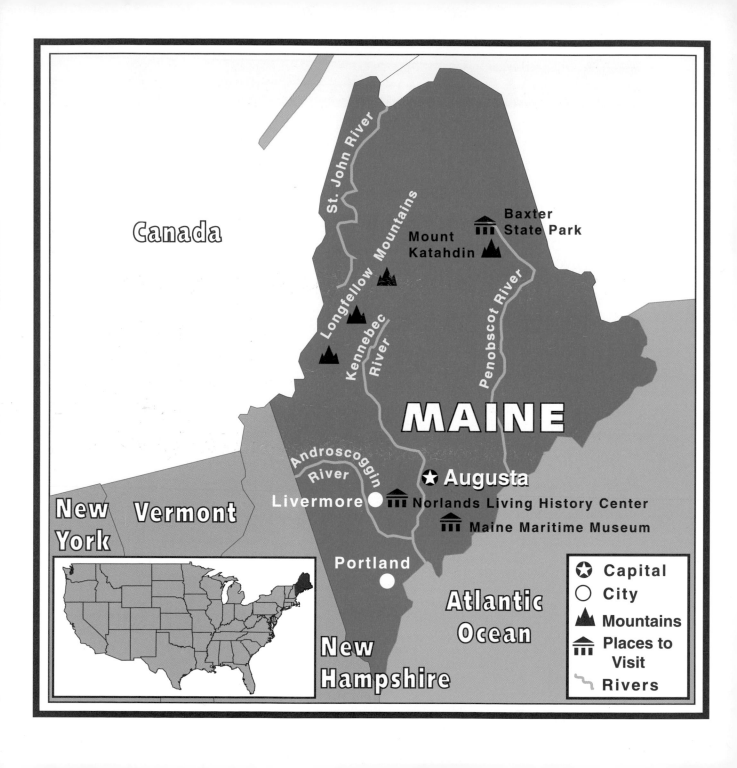

Canada

St. John River

Longfellow Mountains

Mount Katahdin

Baxter State Park

Penobscot River

Kennebec River

MAINE

Androscoggin River

Livermore

Augusta

Norlands Living History Center

Maine Maritime Museum

New York

Vermont

Portland

New Hampshire

Atlantic Ocean

Capital
City
Mountains
Places to Visit
Rivers

Fast Facts

Capital: Augusta is the capital of Maine.

Largest City: Portland is the largest city in Maine. About 64,000 people live in Portland.

Size: Maine covers 35,387 square miles (91,652 square kilometers). It is the 39th largest state.

Location: Maine is in the northeastern United States. Canada borders Maine to the north.

Population: About 1,244,250 people live in Maine (U.S. Census Bureau, 1998 estimate).

Statehood: Maine became the 23rd state on March 15, 1820.

Natural Resources: Maine's natural resources include fish, lobster, limestone, and granite.

Manufactured Goods: Workers in Maine make paper products, electronics, and leather. They also cut trees from forests to make lumber.

Crops: Maine farmers grow potatoes, blueberries, and apples. Livestock farmers raise chickens and dairy cows.

State Name and Nickname

No one knows for sure where the name Maine comes from. English explorers may have given Maine its name in the 1500s. The explorers traveled along what is now the northeast coast of the United States. The explorers visited islands off the mainland. They called the mainland Maine. This name set apart the mainland from the islands that they were exploring.

Some people think English settlers named Maine to honor England's Queen Henrietta Maria. She was married to King Charles I. He ruled Great Britain from 1625 to 1649. Queen Henrietta was the daughter of King Henry IV of France. Henrietta owned a region in France called Mayne.

Maine's nickname is the Pine Tree State. Forests cover large areas of Maine. The white pine is Maine's official state tree. This tree grows throughout the state.

English explorers first explored Maine's coastline in the 1500s.

State Seal and Motto

Maine adopted its state seal in 1820. The seal reminds people of their state's government. The seal also makes government papers official.

Maine's seal has a shield in the center. A pine tree and a moose appear on the shield. The tree stands for Maine's pine forests. The moose represents the state's wildlife. A farmer stands on the left side of the shield. Farming is an important part of Maine's economy. A sailor stands to the right of the shield. The sailor represents the importance of the Atlantic Ocean to Maine. Maine's fishers catch fish and lobster.

Maine's state motto also is on the seal. "Dirigo" is Latin for "I guide." The North Sta appears above Maine's motto. Sailors used t North Star to guide them on the sea. Main believe their state government guides the the North Star guides sailors.

The North Star on Maine's state seal a
Maine's location in the upper northea

State Capitol and Flags

Augusta is the capital of Maine. Maine's capitol building is in Augusta. Government officials meet in the capitol to make the state's laws.

Workers built the capitol from 1829 to 1832. The capitol is made of granite from Maine. Miners removed this stone from shallow pits called quarries.

A large dome tops the capitol. The dome is covered with gold and is 185 feet (56 meters) tall. A statue of the goddess of wisdom stands on top of the dome. The statue reminds government officials to make wise decisions.

Maine's state flag was adopted in 1909. The flag is blue with the state seal in the middle.

In 1939, Maine adopted an official maritime flag. Sailors from Maine fly the maritime flag on their boats. This flag is white with a green pine tree in the center. An anchor lies below the pine tree.

The blue background in Maine's state flag is the same color as the blue in the United States flag.

In 1927, Maine adopted the black-capped chickadee as the state bird. This type of chickadee is common throughout Maine.

Black-capped chickadees are 4 to 5 inches (10 to 13 centimeters) long. The chickadee has a black throat and a gray back and tail. Its belly and cheeks are white. The black-capped chickadee has markings on its head that look like a black cap.

Chickadees eat a variety of foods. These foods include caterpillars, insect eggs, ants, beetles, snails, and other small creatures.

Chickadees do not fly south for the winter like many birds do. During the summer and fall, chickadees hide seeds and nuts in trees. The stored food helps them survive during winter.

Chickadees lay six to eight eggs that hatch in about 12 days. Young chickadees usually leave the nest when they are 21 to 28 days old.

Chickadees have a song that is easy to recognize. It sounds like chick-a-dee-dee-dee-dee.

State Tree

Maine's government chose the white pine as the state tree in 1959. White pine trees grow in forests throughout Maine.

White pine trees grow to be more than 80 feet (24 meters) tall. Some white pines grow as tall as 200 feet (61 meters).

White pines have soft, blue-green needles that keep their color all year. The needles grow to be 3 to 5 inches (8 to 12 centimeters) long.

People have found many uses for white pine trees. Early settlers used white pine bark to make cough medicine. Ship builders used white pine trees to make masts for ships. A ship's sails are attached to the mast.

Today, white pine trees often are planted in areas where forests have been cut down. People use lumber from these trees to make cabinets, shelves, and other furniture.

White pine trees are the largest pine trees in the northeastern United States.

State Flower

In 1895, Maine officials adopted the white pinecone and tassel as Maine's state flower. This flower grows on white pine trees. The pinecone holds the tree's seeds.

Pinecones are the flowering part of a pine tree. Cones on a white pine tree usually grow to be 4 to 6 inches (10 to 15 centimeters) long. White pine tree cones are slightly curved. Their scales are thin and do not have prickles like other pinecones.

The tassel on a white pine tree is a bundle of about 5 needles. Each soft needle is about 3 or 4 inches (7.5 to 10 centimeters) long. Tassels often hang over individual pinecones on a pine tree.

White pinecones also have a fragrant resin. This sticky, yellow or brown liquid oozes from pinecones and other parts of the tree. Workers use pine tree resin to make varnishes, plastics, glue, and rubber.

Maine is the only state with a pinecone and tassel as the state flower.

State Animal

Government officials adopted the moose as Maine's state animal in 1979. Many moose live in Maine's forests. These tall, brown animals have humped shoulders and long, thin legs.

Female moose are called cows. Cows give birth to their young in the spring. They usually have one to three calves each season. Cows can be dangerous animals. They charge at humans or other animals that come too close to their young.

Male moose are called bulls. A bull can weigh more than 1,000 pounds (454 kilograms). Bulls grow new antlers on their heads each year. These large branchlike growths can be up to 6 feet (1.8 meters) wide.

Moose feed on tree bark and grasses. The Algonquian (al-GOHNK-win) Native Americans called these animals mooswa. Mooswa means "animal that strips bark from trees."

The moose is the largest member of the deer family.

More State Symbols

State Berry: In 1991, Maine adopted the wild blueberry as its state berry. Maine farmers grow 98 percent of the United States' lowbush blueberry crop. These blueberries grow close to the ground.

State Cat: The coon cat was adopted as Maine's state cat in 1985. Coon cats are named after raccoons. These cats have stripes and bushy tails like raccoons.

State Fish: In 1969, Maine adopted the landlocked salmon as its state fish. These large fish are native to Maine's lakes.

State Insect: Maine schoolchildren chose the honeybee as the state insect in 1975. Honeybees nest throughout Maine.

State Vessel: Officials named the *Schooner Bowdoin* (BO-din) as Maine's state vessel in 1987. Scientists sailed this wooden ship to explore the Arctic area 26 times.

The lowbush blueberry is shorter than other blueberry bushes. Most Maine farmers grow lowbush blueberries.

Places to Visit

Baxter State Park

Baxter State Park is near Millinocket. The Appalachian Trail ends in Baxter State Park on top of Mount Katahdin. This hiking trail begins in Georgia and is 1,200 miles (1,931 kilometers) long. Visitors to Baxter State Park fish, camp, canoe, swim, and climb.

Maine Maritime Museum

The Maine Maritime Museum is in Bath. Visitors to the museum learn about ships and shipbuilding. From the museum, visitors can take a boat ride past seven lighthouses. Visitors also tour the lighthouses.

Norlands Living History Center

Norlands Living History Center is near Livermore. Norlands is a museum that shows what life was like in New England in the 1700s. Visitors learn about farming, housekeeping, and daily activities of the past.

Words to Know

Arctic (ARK-tik)—the area near the North Pole
maritime (MA-rah-time)—about or near the sea
mast (MAST)—a tall pole on a boat that holds the sails
quarry (KWOR-ee)—a place where minerals and rock are mined
schooner (SKOO-nur)—a ship with masts at the front and back
vessel (VESS-uhl)—a boat or a ship

Read More

Kent, Deborah. *Maine.* America the Beautiful. New York: Children's Press, 1999.
Kummer, Patricia K. *Maine.* One Nation. Mankato, Minn.: Capstone Press, 1998.
Thompson, Kathleen. *Maine.* Portrait of America. Austin, Texas: Raintree Steck-Vaughn, 1996.

Useful Addresses

Maine State Archives
84 State House Station
Cultural Building
Augusta, ME 04333

Office of the Secretary of State
148 State House Station
Augusta, ME 04333-0148

Internet Sites

GeoBop's Maine Symbols
http://www.geobop.com/Eco/ME.htm
Maine Secretary of State Kids' Page
http://www.state.me.us/sos/kids
Maine Symbols: Other Maine Symbols
http://www.midcoast.com/~martucci/flags/maine/other.html

Index